Friends

Friendship is one soul dwelling in two bodies.

[ARISTOTLE]

M·I·L·K™

MOMENTS   INTIMACY   LAUGHTER   KINSHIP

FRIENDS
Copyright © 2007 PQ Blackwell Limited. Published under license from
M.I.L.K. Licensing Limited.
www.milkphotos.com

All copyrights of the photographic images are owned by the individual
photographers who have granted M.I.L.K. Licensing Limited the exclusive
license to use them.

This edition published in 2007 by WPL, The Perfume Factory,
140 Wales Farm Road, London W3 6UG.
www.wpl.eu.com

Edited and designed by WPL
Printed in China

ISBN 978-1-904264-49-1

Inspired by the 1950s landmark photographic exhibition, "The Family of Man", M.I.L.K. began as an epic global search to develop a collection of extraordinary and geographically diverse images portraying humanity's Moments of Intimacy, Laughter and Kinship (M.I.L.K.). This search took the form of a photographic competition – probably the biggest and almost certainly the most ambitious of its kind ever to be conducted. Chosen from 40,000 entries worldwide, the 300 winning images cut across race and nationality and celebrate what it is to be part of a family, to share the gift of friendship and more than anything else, to be loved.

These photographs were first published as three books entitled "Family", "Friendship" and "Love" in early 2001 and are now featured in a range of products worldwide, in nine different languages in more than 20 countries.

M·I·L·K

Wherever you are it is your friends

who make your world.

[WILLIAM JAMES]

It is one of the blessings of old friends

that you can afford to be stupid with them.

[RALPH WALDO EMERSON]

Special times, special places,

special friends together.

The moments pass so quickly

but the memories last forever.

[ANON]

Brows may wrinkle, hair may grey,

but friendship never knows decay.

[JOSEPH PARRY]

Ah, how good it feels!
The hand of an old friend.

[HENRY WADSWORTH LONGFELLOW]

Truly great friends are hard to find,

difficult to leave and impossible to forget.

[G. RANDOLF]

A friend may well be reckoned the
masterpiece of nature.

[RALPH WALDO EMERSON]

One can do without people,

but one has need of a friend.

[CHINESE PROVERB]

True friendship is *felt* not said.

[AUTHOR UNKNOWN]

Friendship is a sheltering tree.

[SAMUEL TAYLOR COLERIDGE]

Many people will walk in and out of your life,

but only true friends will leave

footprints in your heart.

[ELEANOR ROOSEVELT]

The balm of life, a kind and faithful friend.

A friend is, as it were, a second self.

[CICERO]

Laughter is the shortest

distance between friends.

[ANON]

With a friend at your side
no road seems too long.

[JAPANESE PROVERB]

Nothing can come between true friends.

[EURIPIDES]

Hold a true friend with both your hands.

[NIGERIAN PROVERB]

Laughter is not at all
a bad beginning for a friendship,
and it is far the best ending for one.

[OSCAR WILDE]

The most beautiful discovery true friends make is that they can grow separately without growing apart.

[ELISABETH FOLEY]

Side by side or miles apart,

dear friends are always close to the heart.

[AUTHOR UNKNOWN]

Don't walk in front of me, I may not always follow.

Don't walk behind me, I may not always lead.

Just walk beside me and be my friend.

[ALBERT CAMUS]

There is no better $mirror$ than an old friend.

[HINDU PROVERB]

Long friendships are like jewels,

polished over time to become

beautiful and enduring.

[ANON]

May friendship like wine, improve as time

advances. And may we always have old wine,

old friends, and young cares.

[TRADITIONAL]

IMAGES

Two young friends take a break from roller skating on the sidewalk, USA, 1954.
© William Gottlieb / CORBIS

Image not part of the original M.I.L.K. Collection and has been used with the permission of the copyright holder.

Sisters Dorothy and Annie, both over 90, enjoy a quiet moment together. They have taken a seat opposite a country church to watch a wedding party in Owthorpe, in Nottinghamshire, England.
© Steve Hotson

Taking cover – three young friends share the shelter of an umbrella as they wait patiently for an open-air rock concert to begin in London, England.
© Andreas Heumann

Friendship means playing on the same side – a young soccer team in Belfast, Northern Ireland.
© Lance Jones

Coney Island in New York, USA – Six youthful friends turn a sandy beach into a dance floor to the delight of their enthusiastic audience.
© Yorghos Kontaxis

Free fall – four bikini-clad friends leap off a pier into the water below in Miami, Florida, USA.
© K. Hatt

In Warsaw, Poland, Madame Falk's 90th birthday provides the perfect excuse for a tea party. Old friends Madame Malik, 89, and Madame Krauze, 80, share in the celebrations.
© Mikolaj Grynberg

Close companions – William Bossidy listens attentively to his friend John Noonan, a fellow resident at their nursing home in Florida, USA.
© Marianne Thomas

Brother and sister – six-year-old Ethan gives four-year-old Emory an enthusiastic hug at a birthday party in Brooklyn, New York.
© David M. Grossman

The best of friends – Leon and his father, Johnny, take a break from collecting the trash in Jasper, Indiana, USA.
© Tim Lynch

An enthusiastic greeting for a Lithuanian woman on the streets of the old town of Kaunas.
© Romualdas Požerskis

High spirits on the road to Pietrasanta, Italy, as two teenage friends ride to the beach.
© Romano Cagnoni

Conversation comes easily to two old friends as they relax opposite the Shiv Temple of Bilawali in Dewas, India.
© Kailash Soni

Musicians and old friends Ruben and Ibrahin celebrate the release of their new CD at a café in Madrid, Spain.
© Cristina Piza

A retired Canadian war veteran shares a pensive moment with a close companion near Ottawa, Ontario, Canada. Home is an old school bus, which he shares with 15 energetic dogs.
© John A. Hryniuk

Two kilted friends stand out from the crowd at the Gay Pride Festival in London, England.
© Davy Jones

A fashion-conscious trio discover the perfect accessory as they sit in a café in New York, USA.
© Peter Gabriel

Graceful under a heavy load – two Indian women walk side by side as they carry vegetables to market in Calcutta, India.
© Thomas Patrick Kiernan

Summer in New Jersey, USA – best friends Axel and Colby take a break from swimming to cool off with an ice cream
© Greta Pratt

Dancing partners – as two-year-old toddlers Harry and Margaret take to the floor in New York, USA, they can't resist giving each other a hug.
© Darien Mejía-Olivares

Two elderly friends share a joke as they go about their daily work in Chiang Rai, Thailand. They are drying native grass to be made into brooms.
© Pisit Senanunsakul

Bonnie's enthusiastic greeting is matched by a delighted smile from friend Nancy in Washington DC, USA.
© Noelle Tan

An English tradition – deckchairs on the pier provide a typical holiday setting for three friends taking a break in Brighton, in the South of England.
© David Williams

As his friends stride out along a dusty village street near Tijuana, Mexico, a young boy – and his trousers – try to keep up.
© Michael Chiabaudo

In the bright sunshine of Miami, Florida, USA, two friends make sure their noses are well protected as they stroll arm in arm along South Beach.
© Gay Block

An inseparable pair – elderly Ukrainian sisters caught on film during a visit to Cleveland, Ohio, USA.
© Bernard Mendoza

Laughter is infectious for these friends from Mgahinga village, Uganda.
© Malie Rich-Griffith